FUTURE READY PROJECT

FUTURE READY
WRITING
ASSIGNMENTS

LYRIC GREEN AND DANA MEACHEN RAU

Enslow Publishing
101 W. 23rd Street
Suite 240
New York, NY 10011
USA

enslow.com

This edition published in 2018 by Enslow Publishing, LLC
101 W. 23rd Street, Suite 240, New York, NY 10011

Library of Congress Cataloging-in-Publication Data

Names: Green, Lyric, author. | Rau, Dana Meachen, 1971- author.
Title: Future ready writing assignments / Lyric Green and Dana Meachen Rau.
Description: New York : Enslow Publishing, 2018. | Series: Future ready project skills | Includes bibliographical references and index. |
Audience: Grade 4 to 6.
Identifiers: LCCN 2017001300| ISBN 9780766087194 (library-bound) | ISBN
9780766087750 (pbk.) | ISBN 9780766087767 (6-pack)
Subjects: LCSH: Composition (Language arts)--Juvenile literature. | English language--Composition and exercises--Juvenile literature.
Classification: LCC LB1576 .G7398 2018 | DDC 372.62/3044--dc23
LC record available at https://lccn.loc.gov/2017001300

Printed in China

To Our Readers: We have done our best to make sure all website addresses in this book were active and appropriate when we went to press. However, the author and the publisher have no control over and assume no liability for the material available on those websites or on any websites they may link to. Any comments or suggestions can be sent by e-mail to customerservice@enslow.com.

Portions of this book were originally published in the book *Ace Your Writing Assignment*.

Photo Credits: Cover, pp. 4, 8, 16, 23, 33, 37, 40 Ditty_about_summer/Shutterstock.com; p. 3 David Arts/Shutterstock .com; pp. 5, 6, 10, 13, 14, 21, 28, 31, 33, 35 vvlinkov/Shutterstock.com (adapted); p. 7 White Packert/The Image Bank/Getty Images; p. 9 Nukul Chanada/Shutterstock.com; p. 11 Corbis/VCG/Getty Images; p. 13 Ryan McVay/Photodisc/Getty Images; p. 14 Robert Marmion/Alamy Stock Photo; p. 17 GreenPimp/E+/Getty News; p. 19 Tetra Images/Alamy Stock Photo; p. 21 kali9/E+/Getty Images; p. 24 Heide Benser/Corbis/Getty Images; p. 26 Stephen Collector/Photographer's Choice/Getty Images; p. 30 PeopleImages/DigitalVision; p. 34 Robert Burke/Photolibrary/Getty Images; p. 36 antares71/iStock/Thinkstock; p. 38 GlobalStock/E+/Getty Images; p. 39 PhotoAlto/Sigrid Olsson/Brand X Pictures/Getty Images.

CONTENTS

CHAPTER 1

BUILDING WITH WORDS

Have you ever dreamed of opening a candy shop? Imagine streams of eager customers lined up to buy your candy. Imagine the containers of brightly colored candies. Imagine being surrounded by candy morning, noon, and night!

You can't just wake up one day and start selling candy, though. You have to build a shop first. Building is a process with many steps. It takes time, patience, and hard work.

Writing is like building a candy shop. When you write, you need to follow a process, too. At the end you'll have a great piece of writing to share.

A WRITING TOOL KIT

To start writing, you don't need many tools. You just need a pen and paper or a computer, and your imagination!

Computers have special programs that make drafting and revising easier. In word-processing programs, you can easily take out and add words. You can move words and paragraphs from one place to another. You can insert pictures, make the size of words bigger, and even check your spelling!

KINDS OF WRITING

EXPOSITORY
FOR INFORMATION

- Book report
- Science report
- History report
- How-to instructions
- Thank-you note
- Compare and contrast essay
- Opinion piece

CREATIVE
FOR ENTERTAINMENT

- Personal narrative
- Fiction story
- Play
- Poem
- Comic book
- Song
- Myth

THE WRITING PROCESS INCLUDES 5 MAIN STEPS

STEP 1: PREWRITING

The builder of a candy shop has to create a blueprint. A blueprint is a plan for a building. You should also make a blueprint when you write. Prewriting means getting prepared to write. You organize your thoughts in a way that makes sense.

STEP 2: DRAFTING

As she follows her blueprint, a builder puts up walls of wood and brick. You need to build walls, too. A writer's walls are made up of words and paragraphs. Putting the words on paper is called drafting.

STEP 3: REVISION

The walls of the candy shop are up! But there are still fixes to make. A builder makes sure everything is just right—all the way down to the kinds of candy. Your writing needs fixing, too. It also needs flavor. A writer's flavors are the details that make a topic tasty for the reader. Adding flavor is called revision.

STEP 4: PEER REVIEW

A builder's work has one last step. He needs to call in an inspector. An inspector checks to make sure the building is safe and well built. A peer review is when you let others read your work. They give you feedback. Your friend or classmate is your inspector. His or her opinions can help improve your writing. Your peer reviewer can find mistakes that you missed.

STEP 5: PUBLISHING

The shop is done! It's time to sell candy to customers. As a writer, your shop is open when your work is finished. Then you can share your piece with readers. Publishing is a way to share your writing in its best possible form. A builder starts with a plot of land. You can start with a blank piece of paper. Pick up your tools and get ready for some work!

Writing is like building a candy store. It doesn't happen all at once, but the reward is very sweet!

CHAPTER 2

CREATING THE BLUEPRINT: PREWRITING

Should a candy store have lots of windows? Should it be three stories high, or just one? Should it have display tables for the candy? Builders have many choices to make before they start nailing boards or laying bricks. Writers start by asking themselves questions, too. This is part of **Step 1: Prewriting**.

Ask yourself why you are writing in the first place. Then you will know where to start. If your answer is "to have fun," then your piece is probably creative writing. If your answer is "to share information" or "to teach the reader something," then your piece is expository writing. Expository writing describes something, lists facts, or compares things. It can also give an opinion. For expository writing, you might have to do some research. Research is hunting for information about your topic.

Prewriting is an important part of the writing process. This is when you figure out what it is that you want to write.

PLAGIARISM

When you do research, you will discover some great ideas. You might want to put someone else's words or pictures in your own work. If you do this, you must give the name of the person who did the work. Plagiarism is pretending someone else's work is your own. It is against your school rules. If you plagiarize, you could get a zero on your assignment. In college, you could get kicked out of school.

THINK ABOUT YOUR READER

Is your piece a story you want to tell? Is it a poem to read to your classmates? Is it a letter to your grandmother in Hawaii? Think about your reader. This will help you decide what to include. If your writing is an assignment, your teacher might give you a rubric to get you started. A rubric is like a checklist. It tells you what your teacher expects from your writing.

WHAT IS MY MAIN IDEA?

The main idea is what your piece will be about. Try to be specific about your main idea. "Animals" is a broad idea. "Arctic animals" is more specific. The more specific you are, the more details you can give your writing.

SUPPORTING DETAILS

Supporting details are small facts and ideas. They support, or help tell about, your main idea. Let's say your main idea is "Arctic animals." Your supporting details could be "penguins, seals, and orca whales."

Now that you have done some thinking and researching, you can make a blueprint. Writers sometimes use graphic organizers to make a blueprint. A graphic organizer is your writing plan. You don't even need to use complete sentences. Just jot down your ideas. Don't worry about spelling or grammar, just get your ideas on paper.

A Venn diagram is a helpful graphic organizer. It helps you compare and contrast two people or things. You think

Your teacher will give you instructions for your writing assignment. This will help you to create the best project you can.

about how they are alike and different. The Venn diagram on the next page compares and contrasts two kids named Charlie and Allie.

VENN DIAGRAM

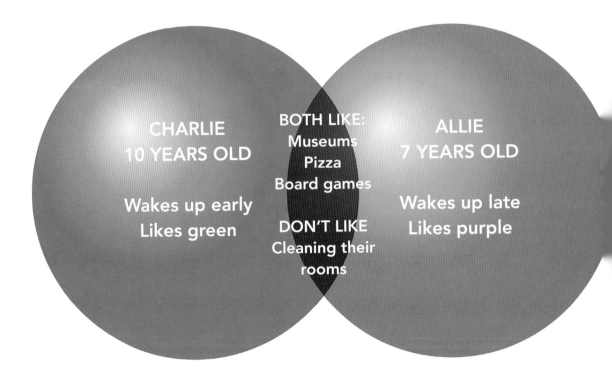

CHARLIE
10 YEARS OLD

Wakes up early
Likes green

BOTH LIKE:
Museums
Pizza
Board games

DON'T LIKE
Cleaning their
rooms

ALLIE
7 YEARS OLD

Wakes up late
Likes purple

BRAIN STORM!

A real storm can be messy. Leaves blow, lightning flashes, and waves crash on a shore. A brainstorm can be messy, too. Brainstorming is making a list of everything that pops into your head. Usually you start by writing down your topic. Then

Brainstorming isn't like a rain storm. But it can give you a flood of ideas!

you make a list of ideas. The list doesn't have to be organized. You can even brainstorm by drawing pictures! Brainstorming can work really well with a writing partner or group.

The 5 Ws are important questions. They work well for expository and creative writing. These help you come up with basic details about the topics and people in your piece.

THE 5 W'S

WHO: my dog
WHAT: likes to eat watermelon rinds
WHEN: in the summer
WHERE: on the porch
WHY: because watermelon rinds are crunchy

ONLINE SAFETY

For your writing assignment, you might have to do research on the internet. Always get help from an adult. Visit websites that are safe for kids. If a site asks for information about you (such as your name, age, address, or photograph), go to another site. Never go to see someone you meet online. If a website makes you feel uncomfortable, close the window right away.

A sequence chart is helpful when you want to tell events in order. This is very helpful for history or science projects.

FIRST, monarch butterfly lays egg

→ NEXT, caterpillar hatches from egg

→ THEN, caterpillar eats milkweed leaves

NEXT, caterpillar sheds skin and grows

AFTER THAT, caterpillar forms chrysalis

LAST, butterfly hatches from chrysalis

Word webs look a lot like blueprints. On the blueprint of a candy store, you might see boxes that show rooms, counters, and tables. Your word web has boxes, too. The main idea is in the center box. Lines come out from the center to more boxes. These boxes hold your supporting details. Each supporting detail needs facts to support it, too. These come off from each supporting detail box.

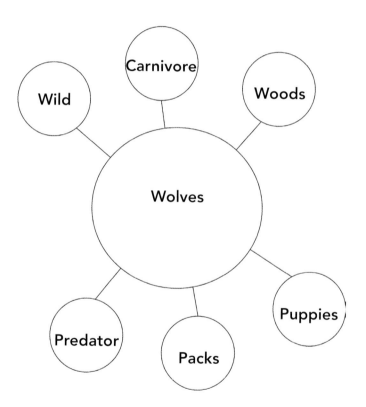

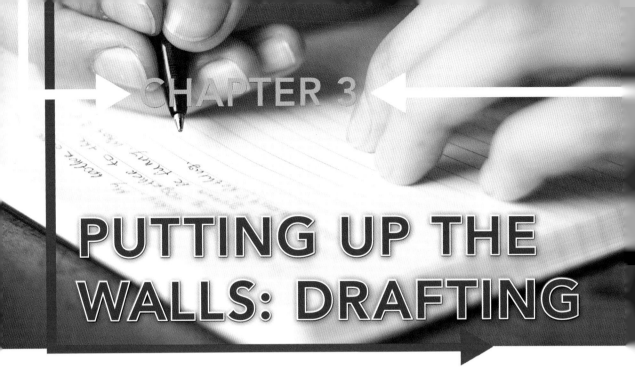

CHAPTER 3

PUTTING UP THE WALLS: DRAFTING

O nce you have your blueprint, it is time to start building your piece of writing. Let's move on to **Step 2: Drafting**.

Imagine that a truck pulls up to the site where you're building your candy shop. It dumps out a huge pile of bricks. Now, pretend each brick is a word. A pile this big is confusing! Which words should you use? Your blueprint is your plan, and your bricks are your words. These words can be nouns, verbs, adverbs, and other kinds of words. As you build sentences brick by brick, your draft starts to appear.

Your words need to be organized in a certain way. In most types of writing, you need to make complete sentences. Complete sentences have a subject and a predicate. The subject is the person or thing that the sentence is about. The predicate tells what the subject is doing or how the subject is feeling.

When you draft, you are **building from the blueprint**, which will guide you in your writing process.

Noun: Armand
Add a verb: Armand baked.

Armand is the subject, and *baked* is the predicate—the action. This sentence looks a bit incomplete, doesn't it? The writer needs to add another word. Some sentences have a direct object or an indirect object. A direct object is the person or thing that the verb happens to.

> *Armand baked cookies. (Cookies is the direct object. Cookies is what the baking happens to.)*

An indirect object is the person or thing the action is being done for. It answers the question, "For whom?"

> *Armand baked Felicity cookies. (Felicity is the indirect object. She is the person that the action is being done for.)*

Now, you can add some adjectives to describe your nouns. This makes your writing snappier.

> *Armand baked Felicity soft, sweet chocolate chip cookies.*

Next, try adding a prepositional phrase. This tells the reader where the action is happening.

When you describe something, don't just think about how it looks. Think about how it smells, tastes, and feels, too.

Armand baked Felicity soft, sweet chocolate chip cookies in the kitchen.

Finally, you can add clauses at the beginning or end of the sentence. Clauses give the reader more information. You can also link two sentences together to make a compound sentence.

When he was here yesterday, Armand baked Felicity soft, sweet chocolate chip cookies in the kitchen, but they were all eaten.

BIGGER BLOCKS OF WORDS

Now that you've organized your words into sentences, it's time to organize your sentences into paragraphs. In creative writing, a new paragraph usually begins a new idea. It can also show that a character is speaking. In expository writing, a paragraph needs a topic sentence and supporting sentences. A topic sentence tells the main idea of the paragraph. Supporting sentences contain the supporting details. See the example below.

The haunted house was scary. Skeletons hung from the ceiling. They rattled when I walked by. One room was black, except for two glowing red eyes. I heard a moaning sound.

ROLLER COASTERS RULE

Roller coasters are the kings of an amusement park. They are the largest rides. They are also the most exciting and popular rides. **FIRST PARAGRAPH (INTRODUCTION)**

Roller coasters are usually the biggest rides at a park. They are taller than all the other rides. Long cars of seats fit lots of people. The lines for roller coasters are the longest. Everyone wants a turn. **SECOND PARAGRAPH (SUPPORTING DETAIL)**

Amusement parks have lots of roller coasters. One is never enough! Even Lake Compounce, a small New England park, has four. Hershey Park in Pennsylvania has eleven. Cedar Point in Ohio has more than any other park—seventeen! **THIRD PARAGRAPH (SUPPORTING DETAIL)**

Roller coasters are the most thrilling rides. You feel like you are flying. You feel scared when you drop down hills. Everyone screams with excitement. **FOURTH PARAGRAPH (SUPPORTING DETAIL)**

Carousels just go around and around. Pirate ships swing back and forth. The Tilt-a-Whirl spins. Roller coasters do it all. Roller coasters rule! **LAST PARAGRAPH (CONCLUSION)**

The first sentence is the main idea of the paragraph. It is also the topic sentence. The other four sentences support the main idea.

The topic sentence does not always have to be first. Look at this paragraph:

> *Birds chirp in the trees. Green grass pokes up through the dirt. I switch my down jacket for a light sweater. These are the signs of spring.*

Here, the topic sentence is the last one in the paragraph. It tells the main idea.

Your paragraphs should also be organized in a certain way. In expository writing, your first paragraph is an introduction. You state the main idea of your whole piece of writing.

The middle paragraphs have supporting details about your main idea. Each paragraph should talk about one detail.

The last paragraph is the conclusion. You summarize what you talked about and restate your main idea.

Before you know it, you've written your first draft! You're not done, though. You can always make it better. A builder might take off his construction hat and take a break … but then it's back to work!

CHAPTER 4

MAKING IT BETTER: REVISION

The walls may be up, but your candy store isn't quite ready to open. **Step 3: Revision** is the most important part of the writing process. Why isn't your draft perfect the first time? Writers are like everyone else—they make mistakes. You want your writing to be the best it can be. That usually means making some changes. Revision is adding words you need and taking away words you don't. You also move words around so they make more sense. Revising is not just fixing a few little mistakes. You might make some major changes.

Try to make your writing as colorful, flavorful, and descriptive as possible. It will not only make your writing more fun to read, but it will also make it more believeable!

ADDING FLAVOR TO YOUR WRITING

A candy shop would be no fun if it only sold red jelly beans. It needs all flavors of jelly beans, butterscotch, chocolate bars, licorice vines, and so much more! Your writing also needs more exciting "flavors." These flavors are details. They make your writing more interesting for a reader. Adding details also helps make your writing complete and understandable to the reader.

When you read your finished draft, pretend you are a reader of your piece instead of the writer. What parts seem to last too long? Do you repeat the same idea? You might want to fix these parts. Try to make them less wordy.

Now look for parts that seem rushed. For example, did you write only one sentence about a very important moment? Take some time to make the moment more exciting. Add descriptive details.

In creative writing, you create your own narrator and characters. The narrator is the person telling the story. The characters are the people (or animals, or plants, or rocks!) in the story. Think about how they feel. Are they happy, scared, angry, or surprised? How can you show these feelings to your reader?

DETAILS

You can also add details by thinking about the five senses. Let's say you are writing about your favorite food. What does it taste, smell, and look like? How does it sound while it's cooking? How does it feel as you swallow it? These details make your topic more real to your readers.

Adding details can also spice up a character's personality. If you write "Oliver smiled" or "Heather smiled," we don't know much about Oliver or Heather. Now, look what happens when we add details:

Oliver's mouth curled up at each end like a snake. His dirty teeth were as jagged as rocks.

Heather's mouth burst with a smile that lit up her face like fireworks.

Adding details is like adding spices to food. They can make the writing delicious!

This sentence could use more details:

Cherry pie is really delicious.

Here is a revised version of the same idea. It has details about feelings, senses, and mood:

My heart starts to pound when Mom takes the pie out of the oven. Golden hills of crust rise above gooey lakes of cherries. The rising steam reaches my nose and pulls me closer as I breathe the sweet air. My mouth begins to water as Mom cuts a slice and puts it on a plate. The vanilla ice cream she scoops on top begins to melt down the sides, creating a beautiful pink pool around the pie. I take a bite. I feel the flaky crust and the tart cherries in my mouth. The cool, sweet vanilla ice cream is so different from the pie, but goes together so well. Then I swallow, and the warmth spreads all the way down to my toes.

MAKE IT MAKE SENSE

Another part of revision is making sure details are in the right sequence, or order. These sentences are in a confusing order:

All the lions of a pride eat together. They stuff themselves with zebra meat.

IN THE WRITING TOOL KIT: THE FLAVORFUL THESAURUS

A thesaurus is a reference book for writers. A reference book gives you quick information. Many computers have thesauruses built in. You can find them on the internet, too. In a thesaurus, you can look up a common word. Then you'll see other words with a similar mearning. This will help you come up with more exciting words. Here are some entries from an online thesaurus:

SCARY: Alarming, chilling, creepy, eerie, spooky.
HAPPY: Cheerful, ecstatic, joyful, merry.
BIG: Bulky, grand, tall, roomy

You can't just choose any word you want from the list. For example, bulky and grand don't mean exactly the same thing! Use the word that best fits your meaning.

A lioness waits in the tall grass until just the right moment. Then she runs after a zebra, pulls it down, and kills it.

Lions are fierce predators. They can kill animals that are faster and bigger than they are.

Lions sometimes drag their prey to a shady spot.

Putting the sentences in a different sequence helps the reader put events in order:

Lions are fierce predators. They can kill animals that are faster and bigger than they are.

A lioness waits in the tall grass until just the right moment. Then she runs after a zebra, pulls it down, and kills it. Lions sometimes drag their prey to a shady spot.

All the lions of a pride eat together. They stuff themselves with zebra meat.

You can use time words to put your facts in the right sequence:

First, we packed our beach bag.

Then we drove to the beach.

Next, we walked out on the sand.

Last, we huddled under the umbrella. It started raining!

The next step in revision is to look at your words and think about better ones. Make sure every word you choose has the right meaning. It should also set the mood you want for your piece. Mood is how you want your readers to feel.

First, look at nouns and see if you can be more specific.

Parker picked up his things.

When you revise, replace the word things with examples that tell us more about Parker:

Parker picked up his slingshot, a deck of cards, and a piggy bank.

Verbs are action words. They help to make your writing more interesting.

Now take a closer look at your verbs.

Thea jumps.

Jumps isn't a very exciting word. How about if Thea springs from her chair? Or she could leap to catch a falling glass dish.

IN THE WRITING TOOL KIT: THE ALL-KNOWING DICTIONARY

A dictionary doesn't just tell you how to spell a word. It also tells you the part of speech and how to pronounce the word. It provides all of the word's meanings. Some dictionaries even tell you what language the word comes from.

Look at adjectives also. You might want to use the word "good" or "happy." But how about telling your reader more? Say "massive mountain" instead of just "big mountain." Don't just say you had a fun day. Say you had a stupendous day!

PROOFREADING

The last step of the revision process is checking for mistakes. This is called proofreading. First, check your punctuation. Do all of your sentences have periods, exclamation points, or question marks at the end? Did you use quotation marks (" ") when people are speaking? Did you indent at the beginning of each paragraph?

Check spelling, too. Make sure to have a dictionary nearby. If you are not sure how something is spelled, look it up. If you wrote your piece on a computer, use the spell-checker. Proceed with caution, though! You still need to read through your whole piece. Double-check for spelling mistakes. You might have mixed up "there" and "their." The spell-checker may not catch it.

Finally, check your grammar. Make sure you use the right form of the verb with your subject. For example, one balloon floats, but two balloons float. Also make sure you use the right verb tenses. The goldfish swam yesterday, but he swims today.

CHAPTER 5

GETTING AN INSPECTION: PEER REVIEW

O nce a building has been built, an inspector comes in. The inspector makes sure everything works. You need an inspector for your writing, too. Now that your piece is written, it is time for **Step 4: Peer Review**. Your peer reviewer gives you feedback. He or she can suggest ways to make your piece better.

SOME THINGS TO KEEP IN MIND DURING A PEER REVIEW:

Was the main idea clear? Did the writer give at least three supporting details? Are all words spelled correctly? Is punctuation in the right place?

Peer review is when you get opinions and advice from a writing partner. Your partner could be a friend or a classmate. Your partner might use a form with places to fill in, such

Peer review can not only make your writing better, but it can also be fun!

as "My favorite part was . . ." or "I think you can make it better by . . ." If your teacher gave you a rubric, your partner might use it during peer review.

A good peer reviewer gives you helpful feedback. It's not helpful to say, "I didn't like the beginning because it was boring." Here is some helpful feedback: "The beginning didn't tell me very much. I wanted to know more about the spaceship."

Now that your partner has given you feedback, what should you do with it? Think about what your partner liked or didn't like. Decide if you want to make some changes. Then get back to work and fix it. You can do a peer review anytime. You don't have to wait until you are finished writing. Ask a friend for help during the prewriting, drafting, and revision steps, too.

PROFESSIONAL INSPECTORS

At a publishing company, an editor is like a teacher. He or she reads an author's manuscript and makes suggestions for improvement. An editor is also like a peer review partner. Authors and editors work as a team to make a piece of writing the best it can be. Your favorite novelist has an editor that he or she works with to create your favorite books.

Consider all the notes you've gotten from your readers. These notes can help you figure out what works best in your writing and what still needs work.

CHAPTER 6

OPENING THE DOOR: PUBLISHING

N ow that your candy shop has passed inspection, it's time to open for business! How do you know when you are ready to "open for business" and share your writing? That is for you to decide. Are you happy with what you have created? It's never too late to fix and revise. Some writers revise several times! But when you're ready, it's time for **Step 5: Publishing**.

LET YOUR READERS IN

Open the door to your candy store, and invite in some customers. Let them enjoy what you've built. That's what publishing is like. Publishing is when an author shares his or her work with a larger audience. The writing might turn into a book, a magazine article, or a website. You can publish your writing, too.

If you follow all the steps to writing, you're sure to do well! You may even find that you enjoy writing.

Start by reading your piece aloud to your class, family, or someone you trust. This is one way to share it. You could create your own greeting card with a poem that you wrote. You could write down family memories in a scrapbook. You could post your article on a website or a blog.

Read your writing out loud. You may find mistakes that you've missed before.

Or how about making your own book? All you need is nice paper and a stapler or ribbon! Many writers keep everything they have written. It's fun to look back and see how you have grown as a writer.

Your hard work was worth it. Now everyone can enjoy the writing you built.

CHAPTER 7

GRAMMAR AND PUNCTUATION GUIDE

H ere are the parts of speech you need to build your piece of writing

Noun—a person, place, or thing. Nouns can be singular (one) or plural (more than one). You can usually make a noun plural by adding -s or -es—but not always. Check a dictionary if you are unsure about how to spell a plural noun.

Proper nouns—refer to specific people, places, or things, such as Tennessee, George Washington, and Sahara Desert. The first letter of a proper noun is capitalized.

Common nouns—refer to general people, places, or things, such as students, school, and popcorn.

    Singular— jellybean, child, fish.

    Plural— jellybeans, children, fish.

Assignment pronoun—a word that takes the place of a noun, such as he, she, it, and they.

Possessive pronouns—show ownership. They include his, hers, its, and their.

Verb—a word that shows action or a state of being. Words such as jump, read, and cry are action verbs. To be, to feel, and to seem are states of being. For example, you can be hungry, feel nervous, or seem unhappy.

The tense of a verb shows when the action takes place. Present tense means it is happening right now. Past tense means it happened in the past. Simple future tense means it will happen in the future.

Regular verbs don't change much in each tense.
Maya loves hot dogs. (present tense)
Maya loved hot dogs. (past tense)
Maya will love hot dogs. (simple future tense)

Irregular verbs have a different form in past tense.
Maya eats ten hot dogs. (present tense)
Maya ate ten hot dogs. (past tense)
Maya will eat ten hot dogs. (simple future tense)
The verb to be also changes form in different tenses.
Maya is very full. (present tense)
Maya was very full. (past tense)
Maya will be very full. (simple future tense)

Adjective—a word that tells more about a noun. Adjectives are descriptive words, such as lovely, yellow, and silly. A noun can have more than one adjective: the round, sticky, red peppermint candy

Adverb—a word that tells more about a verb, adjective, or other adverb. Adverbs often answer the questions How? When? Why? or How much?

> *Red Riding Hood skipped merrily to Grandma's house (tells more about the verb skipped).*

> *We are very confused about the homework (tells more about the adjective confused).*

Preposition—a word that connects one word to another word or phrase. It often tells where something is or where it goes.

> *Examples are over, between, of, to, on, and with. The preposition and the words following it are called a **prepositional phrase**. George jumped over the rock.*

Conjunction—a word that links words, phrases, or clauses in a sentence, such as and, but, or, and so.

> *The dog has fangs, so Chris never runs past its house.*

Interjection—a word or words that express emotion. An interjection can be followed by a comma or an exclamation point, depending on how strong the emotion is.

> *Well, I guess you can borrow my favorite sweater.*
> *Yikes! You spilled grape juice all over it.*

The parts of speech can be put together in many different ways.

Phrase—a group of words with a single meaning. A phrase doesn't have a subject and verb. All the words together can act as a part of speech.

> *The boy with the big hat looks ridiculous ("with the big hat" acts as an adjective describing the boy).*

> *The two girls laughed at the same time ("at the same time" acts as an adverb telling when the girls were laughing).*

Clause—a group of words that has a subject and verb and can act as a part of speech.
Independent clauses—can stand alone as a sentence or be a part of a bigger sentence.

> *Jacob plays baseball with his father every day of*

FUTURE READY WRITING ASSIGNMENTS

the week. ("Jacob plays baseball" is an independent clause with a subject and verb)

Dependent (subordinate) clauses cannot stand alone as a sentence and must be part of a bigger sentence.

Emily uses markers when she draws pictures. ("when she draws pictures" is a dependent clause)

Sentences often combine the two types of clauses.

I can't decide whether I like chocolate more than lollipops.

The first part of the sentence can stand on its own (independent clause). The second part cannot (dependent clause).

Your sentences need punctuation. Punctuation marks help your writing make sense and tell your reader how your words should be read.

PUNCTUATION RULES

Capitalize the first letter of a sentence and put a period at the end.

Replace the period with a question mark if the sentence is a question.

Replace the period with an exclamation point if you want to show strong feeling.

Put commas between words in lists, between clauses, and to set one thought apart from another.

Put quotation marks around sentences that are spoken by a character.

Use apostrophes to show possession (Dana's book) or to make contractions (is not=isn't).

Your nouns and verbs have to agree. That means they make sense together.

Noun-Verb agreement—When a noun is singular, the verb often ends in -s.

The cat purrs all day.

When the noun is plural, the verb usually does not end in -s.

The cats purr all day.

The verb *to be* changes depending on the subject.

I am happy.

You are happy.

He is happy.

They are happy.

GLOSSARY

blueprint A plan for creating something.

brainstorming Writing down everything that comes into your head about a particular topic.

compound sentence Two sentences linked with a conjunction to make one sentence.

conclusion A sentence or paragraph that summarizes a piece of writing.

creative writing Writing with the main purpose of entertaining the reader.

direct object A person or thing that the action of a verb is done to.

drafting Using your prewriting plan to write a full version of your piece.

expository writing Writing meant to share information or to teach the reader.

feedback Someone else's opinions or thoughts about your work.

graphic organizers Charts, diagrams, or other ways to organize your thoughts during prewriting.

indirect object A person or thing an action is being done for or to.

introduction The first part of a piece of writing; it states your main idea and describes your topic.

main idea What your writing is about.

mood The feeling that an author wants to give his or her readers.

peer review Sharing your work with other writers to gather feedback.

plagiarism Using someone else's work as your own without giving credit to the source of the work.

predicate The part of a sentence that includes the verb; it describes what the subject is doing or feeling.

prewriting Organizing your thoughts to prepare for writing. This includes brainstorming, using graphic organizers, and creating a writing plan.

process Something that happens over time, in a series of steps.

proofreading Reading your piece to find spelling, grammar, and punctuation mistakes.

publishing Sharing your completed work with a larger audience.

reference book A book full of quick facts, such as a dictionary or thesaurus.

revision Adding, taking away, or reorganizing words to improve your piece of writing.

rubric A list of what a teacher expects a piece of writing to include.

sequence The order of events in a piece of writing.

subject The noun or pronoun that tells who or what the sentence is about.

thesaurus A reference book or computer tool with entries that list a word along with other words that have the same or similar meaning.

FURTHER READING

BOOKS

826 Valencia. *642 Things to Write About—Young Writer's Edition*. San Francisco, Ca: Chronicle Books, 2014.

Levine, Gail Carson. *Writer to Writer: From Think to Ink*. New York, NY: Harper Collins, 2014.

Randolph, Ryan: *New Research Techniques: Getting the Most Out of Search Engine Tools*. New York, NY: Rosen Publishing, 2011.

Snider, Brandon T. *Write It Out: Hundreds of Writing Prompts to Inspire Creative Thinking*. New York, NY: Sterling Publishing, 2016.

WEBSITES

Grammar Man
grammarmancomic.com/comics/grammarman
Read an online comic about English grammar.

Journal Buddies
journalbuddies.com/journal_prompts__journal_topics/fun-writing-prompts-for-middle-school
Thirty-one fun writing prompts.

Time4Writing
http://www.time4writing.com/free-writing-resources
Find many sources for writing!

INDEX